JEFF GORDON

A Real-Life Reader Biography

Phelan Powell

Mitchell Lane Publishers, Inc.
Bear, Delaware 19701

Copyright © 2000 by Mitchell Lane Publishers. All rights reserved. No part of this book may be reproduced without written permission from the publisher. Printed and bound in the United States of America.

Second Printing

Real-Life Reader Biographies

Selena	Robert Rodriguez	Mariah Carey	Rafael Palmeiro
Tommy Nuñez	Trent Dimas	Cristina Saralegui	Andres Galarraga
Oscar De La Hoya	Gloria Estefan	Jimmy Smits	Mary Joe Fernandez
Cesar Chavez	Chuck Norris	Sinbad	Paula Abdul
Vanessa Williams	Celine Dion	Mia Hamm	Sammy Sosa
Brandy	Michelle Kwan	Rosie O'Donnell	Shania Twain
Garth Brooks	**Jeff Gordon**	Mark McGwire	Salma Hayek
Sheila E.	Hollywood Hogan	Ricky Martin	Britney Spears
Arnold Schwarzenegger			

Library of Congress Cataloging-in-Publication Data
Powell, Phelan.
    Jeff Gordon/Phelan Powell.
       p. cm. — (A real-life reader biography)
    Includes index.
    Summary: Describes the racing career, life, and accomplishments of the NASCAR champion Jeff Gordon.
    ISBN 1-58415-005-X
    1. Gordon, Jeff, 1971- Juvenile literature. 2. Automobile racing drivers—United States Biography Juvenile literature. [1. Gordon, Jeff. 1971- . 2. Automobile racing drivers.]
I. Title. II. Series.
GV1032.G67P69 1999
796.72'092—dc21
[B]   99-24056
                                                                                                                                                               CIP

ABOUT THE AUTHOR: Phelan Powell is a freelance writer who has written several books for young adults. Her titles include biographies of John Candy, Tom Cruise, John LeClair, and Hanson (Chelsea House) and Garth Brooks (Mitchell Lane). A former newspaper reporter, Phelan lives just outside Philadelphia, PA with her husband and two sons.

PHOTO CREDITS: cover: Anthony Neste/Globe Photos; p. 4 Mark Wallheiser/Archive Photos; p. 6 Craig Jones/Allsport; p. 16 Jamie Squire/Allsport; p. 21 Maresa Pryor/Archive Photos; p. 24 Joe Skipper/Archive Photos; p. 25 Craig Jones/Allsport; p. 28 Jeff Christensen; p. 29 Jamie Squire/Allsport; p. 30 Joe Skipper/Archive Photos

ACKNOWLEDGMENTS: The following story has been thoroughly researched, and to the best of our knowledge, represents a true story. Though we try to authorize every biography that we publish, for various reasons, this is not always possible. This story is neither authorized nor endorsed by Jeff Gordon.

Table of Contents

Chapter 1 Racing Prodigy 5

Chapter 2 Trying Something New 10

Chapter 3 Racing Toward Success 14

Chapter 4 Life of a Race Car Driver 19

Chapter 5 Winston Cup Champion 26

Career Statistics 31

Chronology 32

Index 32

Chapter 1
A Racing Prodigy

Race car driver Jeff Gordon often wears a shirt that says "Refuse to Lose." This slogan shows the pressure that he puts on himself to do his best every time he starts an automobile race. Even though no one can win every race, Jeff starts each NASCAR event as if it were the most important thing in the world to finish first.

This attitude has paid off. Before he was 25, Jeff had become one of the most successful and popular stock-car racers ever. By 1998, after only seven years on the Winston Cup circuit, Jeff had earned over $21 million dollars in race prizes.

Jeff Gordon often wears a shirt that says, "Refuse to Lose."

He earns millions more for appearing in advertisements for companies such as Pepsi-Cola. Each week thousands of racing fans cheer him on from the stands or eagerly follow each of his races on television.

Despite this, Jeff remains down-to-earth. He sometimes seems surprised at the attention he has received. "My fans are awesome," Jeff says. "When you see how long they'll wait in a line for an

Millions of fans recognize Jeff's racecar, the Chevy Monte Carlo with #24 painted on the side.

autograph or picture, you realize how much it means to them. I don't think of myself as a celebrity or superstar, so to see people look up to me that way I find overwhelming."

Jeff Gordon certainly didn't come from a celebrity background. He was born on August 4, 1971. His parents, Will and Carol Gordon, already had a three-year-old daughter, Kim. The Gordons lived in Vallejo, California, a town near San Francisco. When Jeff was only three months old, his parents divorced. Kim and Jeff stayed with their mother.

Eventually, Jeff's mother began to date a man named John Bickford. He sold auto parts and was a racing fan. Carol and John would often go to a nearby racetrack, Vallejo Speedway. They would often take Jeff and Kim along with them to the races.

When Jeff was four, Carol and John Bickford got married. That same year, Jeff got his first taste of racing. Bicycle motocross (BMX) racing was becoming

Jeff Gordon didn't come from a celebrity back— ground.

It was Jeff's stepdad who introduced him to racing.

popular, and Jeff gave it a try. However, Carol was worried because she thought BMX racing was too dangerous. She made Jeff stop.

John Bickford knew his young stepson wanted to race. Since he wasn't allowed to race bikes, John bought Jeff and Kim little race cars. Called quarter midgets, the cars were powered by one-cylinder engines. Carol was upset until she realized that the cars were safer than the bikes.

Jeff's car was black and his sister's was pink. Jeff loved his car from the start. He asked John to paint his nickname, "Gordy," on the hood. "We'd take that car out every night after I got home from work and run it lap after lap," John remembered. "Jeff couldn't seem to get enough of it."

When Jeff was five, he was allowed to start competing. His love of driving showed. Even though he was usually the smallest driver on the track, once he got some experience he began to win races. By the time he was eight, he won the national championship of quarter-midget racing.

John knew that Jeff's excitement for racing and his early display of talent could eventually be turned into a successful career. John also knew that he would have to play a big part in setting a path for young Jeff to follow. He took a no-nonsense approach towards helping Jeff. "If you want to be a professional race car driver, you're going to act like a professional race car driver," John told his stepson. This meant that Jeff would have to treat racing seriously. Together, Jeff and John practiced two or three times a week every week of the year.

When he was nine, Jeff wanted a new challenge. He started racing 10-horsepower go-karts. Even though he was competing against drivers who were twice his age, Jeff won 25 races.

In 1981, Jeff won his second national championship in quarter-midgets. It was time for a new challenge.

Together, Jeff and John practiced two or three times a week every week of the year.

Chapter 2
Trying Something New

At 12 years old in California, Jeff was not allowed to drive the larger cars.

Although Jeff had made a name for himself in local racing circles, he had won so many different races that he had basically run out of new challenges in the California area. "You're twelve years old and you have been in the quarter-midgets for eight years," Jeff remembers thinking. "What's next? I was getting older, not knowing what I wanted to do next."

However, he was limited by his age. He could compete in quarter-midgets and go-karts, but most tracks would not allow a 12-year-old to drive larger race cars. To help Jeff, John and

Carol decided to move to Indiana. The advantage of such a major move was that Indiana had no age restriction on track drivers. The family moved to the town of Pittsboro. Jeff's new home was about 20 miles from the track where one of the most famous auto races, the Indy 500, is held. The track, the Indianapolis Motor Speedway is commonly known as the Brickyard.

When he was 13, Jeff started competing in sprint car races. Sprint cars are small and light, but powerful. Jeff had been driving go-karts with 10-horsepower engines. His sprint car had a 650-horsepower engine! Jeff practiced and raced at tracks in Indiana, Ohio, and Illinois. He also raced in Florida during the winter of 1985. Before he was old enough to get an Indiana driver's license, Jeff had won three sprint races against the best competition in the Midwest.

John and Jeff would go to races every weekend. Jeff would first have to compete in qualifying races, called

So his parents moved to Indiana where there are no age restrictions on track drivers.

heats. The top drivers in the qualifying heats would compete in the main race. The driver with the best time in his qualifying heat would start the main race at the front of the field, on the inside of the track. This is called the pole position, and is the best place to start any race.

Randy Kinser, another sprint driver, remembers Jeff's early days. "For being so young, running with good competition on the fast quarter mile, he was doing real well," Kinser said. "He'd race as hard as anybody."

Jeff went to Tri-West High School where he became best friends with a boy named Todd Osborne. Todd's father owned a car shop and it wasn't long before John asked Todd's father, Lee, to build a car for Jeff. "I didn't even want to do the car at first because he was so little," said Lee. "But I figured, as long as he didn't sue me, I'd build it." By the time Jeff was 18, he was driving the 1,300-pound, 815-horsepower car that Todd's father had built.

Jeff went to Tri-West High School where he became friends with Todd Osborne.

Jeff kept up with his grades and, with Todd, joined the cross-country track team. Even at his young age, he knew it would take physical as well as mental strength to have a successful racing career. He and Todd and their other friends had a lot of fun together, too, even though Jeff's normal racing schedule meant he was behind the wheel practically every Friday, Saturday and Sunday night.

Jeff graduated from high school in 1989. That same year, he won the national championship in midget sprint car racing. Unlike a lot of teenagers who at that young age have little idea what they want to do with their lives, Jeff definitely knew what he wanted. His whole life to that point had been devoted to what he loved and racing would be his career.

> **Jeff raced nearly every Friday, Saturday, and Sunday night.**

Chapter 3
Racing Toward Success

Jeff Gordon always wanted to race on the Indianapolis Motor Speedway.

When Jeff was growing up near the Indianapolis Motor Speedway, he dreamed of racing there someday. However, he was also interested in stock car racing. The Indy 500 involves an open-wheeled type of car that travels at incredibly high speeds. It is a more dangerous type of car racing. Stock car racing can be dangerous also. However, the cars that are used are Fords, Chevrolets, Dodges, and other types that you would see driving on the highways. The only difference is that the race cars have special modifications that make them safe at high speeds.

By the time he was 20, Jeff had won more than 500 races. As he became interested in stock car racing, he attended a driving school operated by a former stock-car champion named Buck Baker. "That first day, the first time I got in[to a stock car] . . . I said 'This is it.' It felt big and heavy," Gordon later recalled. "It felt very fast, but very smooth. I loved it."

Stock car racing is controlled by the National Association for Stock Car Automobile Racing (NASCAR). There are two major racing circuits. Young drivers usually start on the Busch Grand National tour. They develop driving skills there. When they are ready, they go to the "major leagues" of car racing—the Winston Cup circuit.

Jeff's first year on the Busch Grand National circuit was 1991. He performed so well that he was named Rookie of the Year. He was still not sure whether he wanted to race stock cars or Indy cars. He won an important title in open-

As he got older, he became interested in stock car racing.

wheeled cars in 1991, the Silver Crown series.

In 1992, Jeff formed a partnership with a man who remains with him to this day, his friend and mentor Ray Evernham. He asked Evernham to be in charge of his pit crew. Evernham assembled a talented group of mechanics. With a year of Busch racing experience and a smart crew working for him, Jeff was ready to break out in stock car racing.

In the 1992 season, Jeff won three Busch circuit races. He also set a Busch Grand National record by winning the pole position 11 times. This success attracted Rick Hendrick, who owned a team that raced on the Winston Cup

Jeff (left) with pit crew boss, Ray Evernham.

circuit. He admired Jeff's talent, and hired the 20-year-old to race on his team.

Jeff's first shot at Winston Cup racing came in the fall of 1992. Hendrick entered him in a race in Atlanta. Jeff made it through the qualifying heats and finished 31st. Although Jeff had hoped to do better, he was excited about reaching the highest level of stock-car racing.

In 1993, Jeff would race on the Winston Cup circuit full-time. His car was a brightly painted Chevrolet with number 24 painted boldly on the hood and doors. His first race of 1993 was a qualifier for one of the biggest stock-car races, the Daytona 500. Jeff stunned the racing world by winning the qualifier, then finished fifth in the Daytona 500. He had arrived.

By the end of the 1993 season, Jeff had entered 30 races. Even though he didn't win any major races, he finished in the top five racers seven times. In 11

Jeff's first shot at the Winston Cup racing came in the fall of 1992.

races, he was among the top 10 finishers. Jeff won $765,168, and was selected as the Winston Cup Rookie of the Year.

"We had a good year," Jeff said. "I learned a lot and I had the opportunity to race with the best drivers in the world."

But even though 1993 had been a good year, Jeff and his team worked hard in the off-season to make sure that 1994 would be even better.

Chapter 4
Life of a Race Car Driver

The Winston Cup racing circuit takes drivers to North Carolina, Virginia, California, Florida, Pennsylvania, Texas and to many more places. Someone who likes to go home to the same place every night is not cut out to be a race car driver. Jeff and his pit team are constantly on the move during the week as they travel to the next race. Becoming a winning driver takes a lot of mental discipline.

"To me, every race I do not win is a disappointment. There seems to be more disappointments than victories in this sport. I know I've had my share,"

The Winston Cup racing circuit takes drivers to many different states.

> "I always take one race at a time. I try not to look too far ahead."

said Jeff. "I always take one race at a time. I try not to look too far ahead. If you do that you tend to lose sight of what is happening now, which, in racing, can be very dangerous."

Thankfully, Jeff has never been involved in a serious crash, but he did comment on the tragedies that struck the sport as the 1994 Winston Cup season began. Two popular drivers, Neil Bonnett and Rodney Oar, were killed within several days of each other as they raced. It was a harsh reminder that traveling at speeds of almost 200 miles an hour is a dangerous way of making a living.

"This is a job," Jeff said. "You can't worry too much about the dangers. And when you've done it as much as I have, you start to get used to the speeds. You're just trying to focus on getting out there and going fast. You don't think about if there is going to be a wreck. You basically have to get in there and do what you do every weekend."

In addition to crashes, a lot of other things can go wrong and keep a racer from finishing. The car may have mechanical trouble. Instead of worrying about what can go wrong, Jeff and his pit team concentrate on the things they can do to improve their chances of winning. Jeff's pit crew, nicknamed the "Rainbow Warriors" because of Jeff's multicolored race car, is among the best in the business. When Jeff brings his car in for a pit stop, the crew changes tires,

Jeff's crew is nicknamed the "Rainbow Warriors" because of his multicolored race car. Below, the team helps Jeff push his car on pit road at the Daytona International Speedway, February 7, 1998.

21

Having a dedicated team helps Jeff win races.

adds gas, and wipes road grit off the windshield. Sometimes Jeff needs a quick drink of water, too. The team can do all this and have him back in the race in 20 seconds or less!

"It takes key people to make things work, and to me, the Rainbow Warriors are the most important part of all this," Jeff explained. "They are an awesome team and the ones who really make it happen. They believe in each other and do whatever it takes to win. That's quite a commitment, so I feel it's important for me to give back that same commitment."

Having a dedicated team helped Jeff to improve in 1994. On May 29, he won his first Winston Cup race, the Coca-Cola 600. "This absolutely is the greatest moment of my life," said Jeff. "This is a memory and feeling I'll never forget."

Jeff's second victory of the season was also very special. It was the first stock-car race ever held at the Indianapolis Motor Speedway. The race on August 6 was called the Brickyard 400. With just a few laps to go, Jeff passed Ernie Irvan to win the race.

By the end of the season, Jeff had 12 top-10 finishes to go along with his two victories, and he had won $1,779,523. But perhaps his biggest moment of 1994 came on November 26, when he married the woman he also calls his best friend, Brooke Sealy.

Jeff met Brooke in 1993. She had won a beauty contest and was named Miss Winston Cup that year. Her job was to give the winning drivers their trophies and kiss them on the cheek. Whatever kind of race Jeff ran in 1993, he definitely had enough energy left to notice the young brunette beauty at the end. "I was wowed before I ever met her," Jeff remembers.

NASCAR and the Winston Cup circuit do not allow Miss Winston to date the drivers on the circuit. So Jeff and Brooke had to wait a year before they could tell people that there was a special feeling between them.

In 1994, Jeff married his best friend, Brooke Sealy.

Jeff hugs his wife, Brooke in victory lane after winning the Daytona 500 in 1997.

After they married, Brooke traveled with Jeff to every race. They attend church regularly together, and try to do things that other young couples do. "Brooke and I . . . like to go out to dinner, see movies, relax at home watching TV. Just being together and having personal time away from the race track is very important to us. We

like to share that time together and not think about racing."

Just being together away from the track is very important to Jeff and Brooke. But, Brooke is at Jeff's side for all his races.

Chapter 5
Winston Cup Champion

The Winston Cup Champion is determined by a point system.

One thing that Jeff was thinking about before the 1995 season began was winning the Winston Cup championship.

Every year, the Winston Cup champion is determined by a point system. Drivers get points for every race that they finish, the position that they finish, and how many laps they led during the race. A driver doesn't have to have the most wins to earn the point championship, he just has to be consistent.

Jeff was very consistent in 1995. He entered 31 races, and finished in the top ten 23 times. Seventeen of those times he finished among the top five drivers. And he won seven races. By the middle of the season, Jeff had created a big lead in the Winston Cup points. Late in the year, Dale Earnhardt nearly caught Jeff. Earnhardt is one of the best drivers of all time. He had won the Winston Cup title seven times, and four times in the previous five years. But Jeff managed to win the title by 34 points. He was the second-youngest driver ever to win the title.

Jeff received $1.3 million for his first Winston Cup title. That was on top of the $2.4 million in race prize money that he won, and another $650,000 in bonuses. His total winnings, $4,347,343, set a circuit record.

The next year was another good season for Jeff. He won 10 races and $3.4 million. However, he narrowly lost the points title to Terry Labonte at the end of the season. In 1997, he reclaimed the Winston Cup title in an incredible season. He opened the year with an

Jeff received $1.3 million for his first Winston Cup title.

exciting victory in the biggest stock-car race, the Daytona 500. By the end of 1997, he had won 10 races, finished in the top five drivers 22 times, and took home $6.5 million in prize money. He repeated as Winston Cup champion in 1998, winning 13 times and finishing in the top-5 26 times. He seemed to be well

Jeff waves to his fans as he stands next to his race car in Time Square, New York on December 5, 1997.

on his way to repeating again in 1999 when he won the Daytona 500 again.

Although Jeff loves to race and to win, he keeps busy off the track. Jeff and Brooke donate money and time to the Leukemia Society of America. He is also involved with Easter Seals and the Make-A-Wish Foundation.

How far can Jeff Gordon go? His more than 40 victories on the Winston Cup circuit already rank him among the

Jeff and his crew celebrate their victory at the Daytona 500 in February 1998.

top drivers of all time. He could be driving competitively for another 15 to 20 years, and break every racing record. "I'm counting on a long career," Jeff says, "and stock car racing is where I want to be."

Jeff listens from the driver's seat of his #24 Chevrolet in the pits at the Daytona International Speedway.

Career Statistics

Year	Races	Wins	Money
1992	1	0	$6,250
1993	30	0	$765,368
1994	31	2	$1,779,523
1995	31	7	$4,347,343
1996	31	10	$3,428,485
1997	32	10	$6,375,462
1998	33	13	$5,158,392
Total	189	42	$21,860,658

Chronology

1971	Born August 4 in Vallejo, California, to Carol and Will Gordon
1975	Carol Gordon marries John Bickford; Jeff receives first racing car
1979	Wins first national championship, in quarter-midget cars
1981	Repeats as quarter midget national champion
1984	Gordon family moves to Pittsboro, Indiana
1989	Graduates from Tri-West High School; wins USAC midget sprint championship
1991	Enters Busch Grand National Circuit; named Rookie of the Year
1992	Signs with Rick Hendrick; wins three Busch races; enters first Winston Cup race
1993	Becomes youngest driver ever to win a qualifier for the Daytona 500; wins Winston Cup Rookie of the Year award
1994	Wins first two races, the Coca-Cola 600 and the inaugural Brickyard 400; marries Brooke Sealy
1995	Wins first Winston Cup Championship
1996	Wins 10 races; places second in Winston Cup points competition
1997	Becomes the youngest driver ever to win the Daytona 500; wins second Winston Cup Championship; becomes first driver to earn $6 million in a season.
1998	Wins third Winston Cup Championship
1999	Wins Daytona 500 for the second time

Index

Bickford, John (stepfather) 7, 8, 9–11
BMX racing 7
Bonnett, Neil 20
Busch Grand National Circuit 15, 16
Daytona 500 17, 28, 29
Earnhardt, Dale 27
Evernham, Ray 16
Go-Cart racing 9
Gordon, Jeff
    birth of 7
    brothers and sisters 7
    charity 29
    early years 7–15
    graduates high school 13
    marriage of 23, 24
    parents of 7
Indianapolis Motor Speedway 11, 14
Kinser, Randy 12
NASCAR 15
Oar, Rodney 20
Osborne, Todd 12
Rainbow Warriors 21, 22
Sealy, Brooke (wife) 23
Winston Cup 5, 16, 17, 19, 22, 26, 27, 28, 29